Hotel abc

Hotel abc

Susan Gevirtz

NIGHTBOAT BOOKS
NEW YORK

© 2016 Susan Gevirtz
All rights reserved
Printed in the United States

ISBN 978-1-937658-57-1

Design and typesetting by Margaret Tedesco
Text set in Adobe Caslon and Futura

Cover photography by Maggie Preston

Cataloging-in-publication data is available
from the Library of Congress

Distributed by the University Press of New England
One Court Street
Lebanon, NH 03766
www.upne.com

Nightboat Books
New York
www.nightboat.org

To the birdhandlers

CONTENTS

CODICIL

— What is not being said
is being repeated

Keep
keep recall
keep harbor
keep
council
keep strength's amnesiac
puncture wound

Recalled
recall
ingrate we were
misled misread by
leaders and guides
collateral damage
has brought us
tourists in our own futures
picked off
uprooted
olive trees
can't suffice
in the near vacuum of space
a feather a rock decoys
equally eyes
warheads or birds
scientific fraud
tell D and mine

I'll send one you can't get
lines
low tides
these long pulling
the _____ out of gravity
went to _____
went to Abbott's Lagoon Closed
the whole world closed up around
you stop swallowing

lighthouse
Closed

went to

these long

low tides

these long like your
pulling the _____ out of

Cinnamon cinnabar where red leaves off
I don't see red I see
the word can't hear hear only

running over
a shadow

to kill killer

Dull tantrum
becalmed benefits
of premature death tooth
        granted
time of day
time of day

Truance
exists dead or alive
so can be "brought to justice"
either way as effigy as body as trophy
alition, coalition

and explanation, ation, had to explain the difference between
text and talk, had to have had

THE IMMEDIATE FUTURE

Stop

have had
are the difference

House calls   Close calls   Cold calls   Will call

Fold the house over get butterfly house

As aluminum was Alu min ium

You became

derivation shadowbox Count Countenance
        Amnesiac Mnemonist   in five minutes
        Insomniac Wireless
        Truance asleep on the bed of seashells

You became the Blister Ship
        acting as a kind of thinking as if
        As If Was Is under beneath

Autistic   Acrostic

Amnesiac   Onramp

neurological storm   diagnosis deposited in backseat basket

Dragnet Hex we walked on a dock and jellyfish appeared
dragnet The masts of ships without hulls
dragnet kitchen to be seen but not to see to be blinded by being seen
        Then as
          usual you
           out of the shelves of babes
         a book I've always wanted
               as torso
             forgotten title misfire

dragnet Offshore countries company's continuities stacking cramming false scheduling electrical gaming
dragnet Zenith Ingrate on the day of anagram the known recalled recall
dragnet Trying to say something is sharecropping

PAYLOAD

    Exit Siecle
    Century   *///*

QUANTITY'S TRUANCY

Virgule   Vaudeville   Cognate   Underwater Sound

Joyopolis Theme Park

                                     and after the third day of the fortieth year
                                              I'd had Enough of enough

                                   music without words
                                   music w/out words

                      what they asked for
                        what they got

                                        sometimes in words
                                             they fly up

                              Sometimes   Predator

"vast armada of sleek jet fighters" "unmanned drone"
sun-illumined name
                flown by remote control at the slow speed of 80 mph

              Taking

live video: a mosque, a private residence, a temple, a kitchen, a church, a cemetery, the Kaaba, the tabernacle, the broken hand of the arm of the state, the marketplace, a plate with the remains of a meal

A convoy   leader

                a body, custody, a deal, a plan under the terms of the original agreement lost in sixty seconds

The call went out   But in words

mourning Deployed before

  at the ready

And after the 10th non-biblical year I'd had

enough too

In every conceivable crucible of time

In every uncontainable measure

                non   syllabic

                patterns of consumption

The ceremony of subtraction celebrated
as if its deaf music could be
eyes upon which rain, shine, famine and sleep deprivation

                ignore the ignored

making matrimony of history

as if to go on proclaiming believing

They meet each other

Co-temporality mincing

knower over another

Frontal

verb mimics production

favors knoweth   [over] predilection

MEMORANDUM DRUM

Hunger

/

Overt

        magnet   invitation

Steal to feed
Store up to starve a third

By the way the babes
are kept in a crypt
nursery bureau of incubation

peer through the narrow glass slat

mail the orb of head
gesturing towards a book

        A mistake may walk

        without consent

          x
   XX   xx

as 3 changed minds   feed

complicit   cleptocracy

see how unfinished he was. See how curtailed

              I am no test case

              but the aftertaste of experience

              leaves a residue of explanation

              sighting birdwatchers glare evidence

                                          Attempt

      Ablaze

On Orion

            Do you   the you of imagine

CODICIL

From
from
scratch
from flat line
From geyser range
From breadth's length
From iteration's version   conversion
From "brutality of innocence"
the "just" personal
From the too late beginning
methods of refusal
of refund
defunct
From memorandum drum
Memorabilia done
A.K.A. address plaque
From the answering question
supplanted by
the governing question

        Stop

            Not

                        Stop

   Laid out on
        reverse Esperanto

            R T M A R K

            E T O Y

From the curators

    by teaspoon
    by thimble
    by eyedropper   (fed

SCEPTER OF THE MARKETPLACE

The conditions of problems
The clocks that time us

Roll-A-Way Homes

Wireless

Wireless "beyond measure"

"surplus of care" — Benjamin Hollander

or be like death unworried about
outcome
not like time "parsing its gifts"

in the trenches
in the outback
is the problem
has nothing to do with
why is the

plastered with photos so that the actually person
couldn't approach or be seen even if the dead could walk into the room

DRAGNET

<u>Voltage</u>
<u>Voltage</u> No identifiable bite marks
<u>Voltage</u> Workers drag the bottom of exhaustion
<u>Voltage</u> Inborn ear perhaps velocity shed weight
<u>V</u> "that by which we are no longer able to be able" — Blanchot
<u>V</u> Livid city red cross
<u>V</u> Come   #   Here   #   Oren

       Beg

           plunder in Ramallah
<u>V</u> Home again home again but then
<u>V</u> Livid city ellipse City caesura City pause hesitation lacunae Metropolis
masturbation = mourning

      in a little box bed

      echo demo so
    a way to miss / tryst of worst
          a little wend way shed
<u>Voltage</u> Foreshade accompany that body

       Water of sewage drank

     Water of all the seas from deduce
      one member/we given/under

Statement as testament of
offers the speaker
a momentary respite from supplement

       Water scourge sank
      waker of the seas
      of all the seen   worker

         oh all across
        oh accursed the darkened
        accused

<u>Voltage</u> Quadrangle refusal

TRAILER
sated square

Oh   what was his name
              wasn't there
      I was younger by then

                        all the gates
            curfew
                  a salted measure
        ten years later

      time hasn't had
              its day

[anniversary of Rodney King verdict, broadcast 10 yrs later]

UNDERWATER SOUND

Got light

not bought but as means of occurrence
means means of occurrence

more paraphernalia for distant proximity:
    cam camera   sister suicide bomber

The future you asked about is a square torn out
    of the center of gold and orange money for the dead

        no smog   no weather
They stand on a land of magnet dirt

under
    Overpass

Cognate
    [rebate]

                entry gratified
                granted /

                    /

                    that we

DRONE

thousand minute years ——

world not

s   plurality

                             was copying. was
     running through a wood copse. I was
system to system
was. . . . . . was

was scrabble sent

scramble writ

scriven drive

[unplanned   untimed and untimely]

squabblement

25

Bossed around   sure as ruse

FAUX PRESENT   unyoke your oxen rockets

They are not

  you   balancing a needle

on the nose

of a generation

          who is the mother of damage
          who is the handmaiden

dustless black pepper

household hammers on nuclear warheads (Berrigan)

Remember

JOYOPOLIS THEME PARK

No   I meant
          except that's in
          the middle

excerpt as norm exception

No, I said

POSSIBLE

KIM POSSIBLE
So not the drama

      Greed disclaimers
        Alert letters
          Gauntlet's adolescence
Wake up when it's over Seaworld
      watchtower in the parking lot
      embracing strollers

Now I know, Ron Stoppable
      buy me initials
      under arrest concession
      snow cone suspicion
colder and older grows the hot day

Now I must wash my too clean body Prepare for the pile of teeth served by the
dentist Always in trouble with information Recall as a form of public speech
Unapproachable unachievable And now must hang myself in the doorway of false
distinctions

No outcome

outcome

outcome

LINER NOTES

Argument

        The stories of disappearance were
are not true
Made to appear to disappear
One way street to the museum   =   repatriation
Brain removed   sent to the Smithsonian
How did he become undead so that he could be reburied?

        A member of a remnant

        A body suitable for salvage

His state of undress a state of dress
Image as provocation not dead body

((((((()))))))

objects _____ and throw them back

    says something about something they've talked about

        [not your victim your conscience]

What does this situation

        [the difference between mediums is timing

No dates   No circa   Unmade bed   vent

Provoke: "We're out in the world and we see something"

Electric raids   Cotton in my ears   I could still hear

— James Clifford and James Luna in performance and "conversation"
October 2002 California College of Arts and Crafts

28

MINUTES OF VENUS MEETING

Preface to the Hebrew Translation (1939), re-edited 1955

"What is not being said has already been repeated"

You are broken?   Any answer

over-implicates

a past

Let's be archaic. Let's melancholy our UFOs. Let's give them names of the gods.
Let's call it custodial. Let's get fired. Let's starve the pets and leave the house. No,
leave the poets and feed the harbinger of the atmosphere. When they suddenly
disappear the cardinal directions
"The medulla oblongata is a very serious and lovely object" — Freud

Locutions of the anticipatory: The first Schtetl Program

Way up in the sky

Prophecy is anxiety taken through the outer splinters of fear to the reassembled
landscape beyond

unconsummated pre-verbal writing
and so the interruption of excitation

Again

As careful as the first lightning was
when it made its first fire

As careful as

Each day   then each next day re-set

so in the dark "If someone speaks it gets lighter"

enough time spills that

planets hijack their own trails

I mean

    stain that is a continent

    lend me your shape

    so I too may become

        the thing unforeseen

SCRIPT FOR RADIO

But it's not the relatively commonplace discovery of a Neolithic skull, dating from the third millennium B.C., that so astonishes us today. It's not even the fact that the skull, upon examination, turned out to be trepanned. It had been carved open, apparently with the aid of a rough flint — a primitive crown saw — and the brain had been operated on for an estimated period of three hours. The whole intervention had left a cicatrice nine centimeters long. No, it's neither the black skull nor the jagged scar that runs like some kind of virulent root about one side of the skull plate that so fascinates us today, but the ear, the artificial ear, that once locked into the left side of that hollow, black receptacle. Carved from a seashell, the *spondylus Graederopus*, its artisan had used the shell's thick hinge to replicate the earlobe and its shallow vault to imitate the concavity of the ear's outer whorl.

— Sobin, Luminous Debris

Glory! Until yesterday I didn't know it in its indisputable essence, and from now on nothing else so-called will ever be of interest to me.

— Mallarmé, "La Gloire"

It digests, repeats, re-writes, comments upon itself. Unattributed quotes indicate either a decision to leave speech detached from any one original speaker, author or issuance, or they mark the 'as if' — the place where that which is in quotes might have been said, rather than where it is, or was, definitely said — A kind of hijacking of attribution — Instead to locate the uncertain, the hesitation, the provisional — what might exist before or after the page — That which might better not appear on the page at all, and having landed there anyway, what might gesture toward the off-page world, the margin of indecision in which the assumption of a writer writing, of a "community" of reading writers, the question of what those might be, is under examination, invoked and under invention — Thus the reoccurrence of titles and lines.

Not all deaths make noise but this one did and that echo preceded his actual fall. This is the way the sonic moves issuing from so many directions and sometimes before the source.

"I am breaking into bodies like a bank"

— Eleni Stecopoulos

I am broken into by sound

What showdown what impasse what constellations of form's presentations as corral zoo barn are not my chosen vocation

Form's reason times motion's delineation as distinct as X times X as the end of the movie exit sign of the theatre sudden end of N's speech as her voice and our talk continue yet the impasse of silence of the body gone astray cannot be underestimated, as true as sonnet

Saying something does not necessarily look like saying. The necessity of address creates a necessity of kind of address, a violation of other kinds of address — So <kind> registers the address and its urgency. The words of the address itself a demonstration of a demonstration of kind

"What we knew as children, we now must grope for because sight and sound have fallen apart."
                    — Hornbustel in Jakobson, *The Sound Shape of Language*

Acousmatic longing in the body groping toward nostos to hearing reading, a hearing, in which the one on trial is "the said" and the interruption of saying enters as the brain's surgery on itself

Before I had ever read or heard of the word *gloire* it began to make its visitations. It would not go away and it led the way. Repeatedly it woke me from sleep. It stuttered over dishes. It broke itself apart and reassembled its syllables, phonemes, letters, amoeba-like. Sometimes its glitter background held the air up where it would have otherwise caved in, a tent missing poles. Other times it matched the ambulance siren and could only = emergency. Its insistence upon a state of the bright vociferous that words and the under-heard can sometimes beam, regardless of tone, was a repeating interruption.

Much later, on excavation and as revelation, it turned up in Mallarmé's essay "La Gloire":

"A hundred posters absorbing the uncomprehended gold of the days (treason of letters) flew by, as if to all the outposts of the city, my eyes being drawn to the horizon's edge by a departure on the rails before being gathered into the abstruse loftiness that an approach to a forest in the time of its apotheosis bestows."

— Mallarmé, "La Gloire"

the "treason of letters" against letters — betrayal is to *not* grasp "the gold of the days"
without anachronism, by the ear of "blind listening" we return and proceed —
who, is also as usual, the object of desire

and the one whose only remains are his Will and Testament

"In 1932 Roman Jakobson presented in his essay *Musikwissenschaft und Linguistik* the following hypothetical situation. An African musician plays a bamboo flute. A European musician has various difficulties trying to reproduce the exotic melody but eventually he manages to establish the height of the tones. He plays the melody in the belief that he represents the music accurately. The African denies this because to him the European does not pay sufficient attention to the colour of the tone. Then the African musician plays his melody using a different flute. The European perceives it as a different melody because the relations between the heights of the tones are different with the new instrument. Yet the African swears it is the same melody. Jakobson concludes by stating that in music *the given* does not count. It is the *conceptualized* that matters."

— What is not being said
    is being repeated

BROADCAST

If only I could run my tongue

       Etc
    & inside

but such bewildment

   last time you beheaded that

poss.   — would it
         be same

     Explanation

   The mundane   gauntlet

 Or

Once upon a time I was molested by a pedophile

    The Fable of the Ascetic and the Hedonist

A fit of optimism

Supplanted by

      A book called S P O K E

      A book called T A L K

GLOIRE <^>
     The L's talk to each other

glory, gore and glare on a long distance conference call

00.5   the claque   the hired clappers

00.33   Pantagruel's radio

00.48   sounds off the sea consist of words frozen in the winter air

00.04   as our ship enters air, they thaw thus becoming audible

00.1   "And we could see sharp words (which according to the pilot, sometimes went back to the place where they'd been spoken, only to find the throat that uttered them had been slit open)"   — Rabelais

That the words were hung upon is true

    That they hung is also true

    bitter injection below the frame

    You get all the sounds. Even the ones I don't make

Theme without gravity

Fast action without report

      Miscalculus each   miraculous match
Execute association   wave sine wave   all we land upon is
Breath through the cracked door

of morning   of furlough

      Furlough at Gloire

      Doubletalk

on the cutting room floor

       Name which

      There you go find there

      Something dust

A

As in umbrella

2 as in immense

    2 as in mistook

and pivots around this until this is dislodged

      this is double announcement

have they their cities

                Allegedly

has one year yesterday from moving out

    Allegations

Spoke the middle tongue

    took the forked road

Offer no bail

 line

      CLATTER

Have no

   Ire

   Little sheep

      Gone to bed

    in kitchen shed

   cut and dice and wake up handling

Have no
   Sleep,   Little
Cradled by
Crossed out
Sun

Not thematic under the thumb of

    The cracked door

"We've gone so far into the future that time has started over again"
— The Flintstones

                    what would if
                    that there were
                  skewered on
                    news

        Last February
           Friday

Reductio ad Electionem

One-track mind headshot

The Book of Halts

The Announcement Park

The eternal Table of Contents

        He can do   what will does   what reason

Has he   arms way

Drink of early mind reader

        Non ex-murderer

upon the true
Ramparts

Who was the driver

And how was the ambulance making it through

Touch Infra-Red   Metal detector white

        All new names for the already named and heard by fingerprint
first
            Density of locatives

        Garden of report

Whispered in line and lines — as line up

As salt is the quickest way to alter anything
Then whispered announcement likewise tills the air

There were door to door weddings, sidewalk sales, shoe shine pavilions,
bumper car graduations, sex in hotel lobbies, as the color wheel changed
its names

What is hardest
or impossible
is to live without address
So we listen   psycho & echo   a dialogue

        -Do you not see that my glare would be
            toucht by your seeing me again?   — Duncan

Terrestrial

Traffic Directing School

A e I o   aeion   Eidolon of Aion or E?

as in Pretext   or dentistry

Hectare: Pound of Distance

[inwish] want and its limits

Corpus Alpha (you) show the alphabet (body)

Telephone Attack

Mapless Atlas

Somnia, my Gloire

Hand Held Density

Ultra-sonic   seen mid-air

The anti-penultimate person   the sacrificial

Chain mail bikinis   solitude
again

                        Gloire |__ Stake   STAKE

                    S L A Y |__   Telecast
                                |__
                                  |__

Our Accomplices

encryption equals inventory by sight

whose compulsive ear does not stop calling

Troubling indications   PSAs   Rewards for the recovery

Charged with the phantom of liberty lost

 October 1, 2000

This state of emergency

or the big break

"which might be the first time I felt it, the corpse itself, in months and months and months"

Feb 21, 2002

That
   those voices in your head may be real

That
researchers have developed a beam of sound so narrow that only one person
can hear it, "Directed" audio sounds like it's coming from right in front of
you even when transmitted from a few hundred meters away.

Shocked!

even more so:

Enlight and conship ent some undernity

then the wind in the weather report itself
leaves the weather lagging behind

cancelled the notice gave notice unnoticed

Got your cells memorized!

Infomercial: What can I say except

that my own sense of crisis still demands

an inventory

     of our mundane bodies

     incomplete as I suspect them to be   I once felt hooked up

to those beautiful machines that knew oh so well how to breathe. This is
also encryption

March 3, 2000

Announce   Abjection

A competition

2 minute memories   the flimsy body of bodies

CUE   take our cue from the rescue workers

July 26, 2001

regardless. or full of regard.

Re:morse

I was somehow able to open up the picture called "bench built of fog"

loud and clear

     that one kind of machinery bred another,
silly to excise

                    I had thought

                         or excuse

               an animal that operates by remote control

               a movie forged from metal

Here we fall out of talk   Showing what's at stake.

More on crisis and rhythm:

— of segue

— of track

— of scavenger hunt

— of beat

— turning out to be the heart

— Is the sleight of hand used to maintain sleep the trick that makes sleep
  look like wakefulness?

— The bonfire -repression of sleep by flame

— Tip the scales

— Sleep without maintenance or goal

— Lever   rotates in opposite directions around the fulcrum

— crisis   this is obviously built in

— switch plate   as in keeping track

The fable of the DJ and the Hedonist

said the reporter on the ground

From the dungeon

trying to ease content

false friend approach

ostensibly getting people to say less and speak more

The Master of Ceremonies Announces

Acoustic Gloire: The Off World talks

          Excoriation Tales

There is remembering that is not recollection

Tectonics talk of

Acoustic fleece   Gloire Fleece

GLOIRE Re Lore

Allotment Gloire Course

There is voyage that is not

Repeating that is not tradition

Tell

per capita

Soon you will have forgotten where it came from, how it arrived here, and
believe it is your own
It will be yours. Like all arrival origin lost in

The Ready

Pitfall — Give them special powers so that their absence is a relief from that
giving

Parting Shots — from the first twenty-four hours:

"Sitting on G waiting for O"

1st memorial notes:

Elaboration the only question
as in freighter arrives
But no one knows how to unload
this cargo

small comfort to the small

dissect propositional preoccupations

insect small comfort

Sacred scare
grove

Restored

The reports are blue lines on the air

The blue lines crosshatch the view

sound without source

is a light rail transom

I hear the smoke of a cigar

I hear the literal translation

Once bones could talk

now smothered in the sacrificial fat of years

bulk up durations and amplitudes

where human face falls away

    Toward it

anti letter

that the questions

Revolve
Sonorous object

conch

picked up

first

before

curtain transmission

Economy
              lifts its

                        head

Looks

and look alike

its pen pal

after the awning

of cutting

reduces

us   to

If only

I could

part the curtain

you would see that the

bellowed   modulated

pins dream

to tactics that won't wake

nor kiss beheaded beloved

Once   off to the disciple life

that celebration of populace fleeceless

CIRCADIA

The meal you serve is a long road
— Loring Danforth

Lustrations, trance locutions __

The glory or halo it who is fire

    an oil lamp on their tombs

    not put out by wind

    is the twin of wind

meteorite stone idol mother of the mother of gods

    cast down

        If you could touch

It would be a starling migrating

    even by dim sun

or from inside a dark glacier

migration itself you could see

          pent-up fire not yet lit

Then the child holding the candle

    same as the candle

The radiance

The filaments kept secret

from jealous siblings the dead

or the first swim of summer

They can never not mourn
They are overjoyed by mourning

They are never not looking

for the surprise of a full tomb

Gifts of sea blue and pomegranate
    crimson — if you could hold it

    a light bulb in a nest

Then we're left with nothing but season

       broken sand

missing   term

     who   roughshod

         covenant

If you could

it would be   [the blow from the sky]

while the sun beats hard underground

       mute
       like math

carted around forever in the guise of
one deficiency, inability, albino, or

it's just attachment to the low-caste state
of preverbal lack of access

A small warm bird
singing at the top of its lungs

doesn't even stop

when the sky

always cracking up

covers their heads

electrocuted thorn sunset
   rest torn from

     those on

       the Devour and Ravenous tour

          faceless kleptos
               zero-in birds of prey

           tooth and crave
             have it all to yourself

        dark clutch

Now to sleep, sweet silverware in a drawer

   shut-up by the shock of plenitude

Your somniloquy and teeth grinding
never done

and so our love

    hunger abated by a fictitious meal

       Radiant in rest
we stenographers of glandular mutter

brain cave our bed
as our heads orbit
bodies stay enrapt

inject hypnotoxin from sleep-deprived dogs into goats
and sleep comes

muscle paralysis keeps the dreamer from gymnastics

Swallows inside the café

and in the cat's teeth

At each signal on the highway

we serve locomotion's claustrophobe

The Bright Beneath Above

"Sleep is for pussies." This vet from the war in Iraq was in my house bragging that she doesn't need sleep. Social productivity training starts in the military, families, and schools — then filters out into the rest of the population. So this is a firewalk for her and all of us casualties of prowess and grooming.

Heed this heathens who attach to the effigy of the human face: some of us were weaned on sound and the sight of a crowned scroll ceremoniously taken out of its cupboard, its purple velvet, unrolled and read aloud. Idol worshippers feel the wooden eyes of an icon following even when they turn their back. The worship of the carved or painted face with its animate eyes versus the worship of the faceless, read aloud and sung over? Both being original and returning objects of love. That *versus* is too severe but still — how do these formative sights impact the way other faces and sounds are forever after imbibed? Idol worshippers drink imago, but it's not like others don't partake of idolatry. Everyone attempts to find the clavé in their waking and sleeping, breathing and pulses. And if you don't search for it, no matter — it will find each of us under the inescapable command of circadian beat. Maybe it's the guise of that circadianity that we call love when we see it in one another's submission to being under the same sun?

Think of the way a spring curves but doesn't touch itself on each return. Of waking and sleeping. Think of the inhaling, exhaling, spinning lower vertebrates of artist Shih Chieh Huang that show us the shape of air and confront us with eyes of those from undersea. Even these, in what Huang calls "The Bright Beneath," are under its thumb. No one escapes circadianity. Except maybe love tries. Or maybe love is our union in circadian service.

Does the vet wish to turn herself into an icon? Or even more into one? If yes, how did this wish come to be hers?

Also, cheap imitation of a form, for example — a volta — the turn without the sonnet
— But   — Yet   — And yet

If it were possible for sections to occur in a shape that keeps revisiting itself, a spiral staircase or ferris wheel in the night, they might be titled:

Volume's Fate
When the Storybrokers Break
Brainstem Flowerer

A letter in bold indicates a new inhale or circa

So come. Let the unwinding begin
— Bioluminescence on land
A festival of "lower" vert and invertebrates, fungi, birds — their love letter.

my emmory

    how escape

rote that

teaches hate

or Each word a final approach

wide wreath

and leave the flash cards behind

Speaking slightly another tongue   Your call

ldve sueep wxlves

      shalt now   change one letter of

            All

be tender tough legible and prophetic   Rove

returning with cinnamon, cardamom, cloves from the spice route Apples
from the old orchard Caravans of ice cream from goat herds led by camels
walking for days on newly paved highways of glass

What do we know of glass roads?

What can we say about routes no longer not yet traversed

What is known of street life on frozen pavement casting glare — Of TV on all night to keep prey outside its circle?

Already written

rounded the wagons up

and in we walked

Darkness   Light   darkness dividing

hair   a telling

a walking

through
        lying down against

on my side this time

the song of no possessions

having given up possessing to have

one of the higher bower

bitten unstrung melody

of high lyric's earthquake safety

Blowjob pass time

Ungraven /

gerund reflective

cannot recall

names of things or people

verbs and their proper declination

as out of reach as

sun blizzard

words only face only

there are no

Already written

snowcaps

on the sea

day escalates

one break

at a time

from lists   "order"

[etymology also causes things

For you

a kernel of normal

a nugget of dust

a filling   a filing   a hand around a kidney, liver,

viscera encirclements
a laying on of

a falling to
          a coming to   and not even singing Yet

pre song

   late in the game

Past bedtime

      beyond daylight savings

telling concealing leaving out prophesying
— to me and not   — to the other but not the place holder

— believing belief to be believed

Do you go there?   late at last

hearthless pledge

child to air & meals   him from the outer door apparition\\appearance bound

Sleep's pledge

wake upon
wake beyond waking

return the minds
of many men shunned

Come back
to bed

Phone call the 2nd

You the great chameleon

the king of them   that all aspire

to resemble

———————
———————
———————

rage pudding
medicine
miracle
believe return manacle

I say this

what works / beast of love /causality of care

I say boastful night bound to stars

causality car

You bring them all close in candy ear
autopsy meds
You strike your match tent

and fire cartwheels all over
our unshared past face

You You   can't stop or cease or

wouldn't because

roller coaster flames

blows us up on

Pressed to

    liver   lung cunt tongue spleen

     our molecular hive of

     makes its own seep

work that out my love
in over and out flesh

whose
tears torn from thorn fronds

     or gator-wading through piranha swamp

yes to the 10th power of volume's fate
yup the lap of stamping through
called tendril filigree under water

then blossom up
        calligraphic in sweet heart of coinage
           I give you coinage

————
————
————

We dress in color

    wash in milk

  do what can

  are done to

Tendon of call

    Call of

                the circadic

              cardiac

     aspirin hours   tonic

if with it
you take

        me without thought

Plague of following eyes
or supine they rest
carried on the backs of the cult of memory
while others busily count the alphabet rosary
to read to hear to read but not see
to light candles before it to it by it
while the book never rests
carrying the act of it is
its own supplicant advocate procession

                    I do not venerate
                    I do not adorate
                                    I repeat

Up all night conversing with
the kibitzers

Up all night storing seeds
for winter

Up with the night revealing seamless stitches
platitudes of clay and bakelite asking
what sustains a sentence

On what is a sentence served

live awash in a sea

gift meal command

overheard the sight of watch
eyes of the words flail to see it
beseech scar tissue
whose density has more visibility than a field for playing Mayan pitz

Then a scroll presented as the real meal
makes exes of all the supplicants
recall what was promised
by way of the counterpart of cancel
and by the same token it is not by eye
that the future beholds us
in this way sight imitates discovery
in others of the inert
but here by the lamp lit on his grave
casting overlap where fire = icon of air

speak to me in wood
mute in dream
but awake in the beheld
and the face held above their heads

carried by the act of _ _ _ _ _ _ _ _
hearing the sight of

overheard the sight of watch
in fact woods waking dream

severed   *repeat*   *echo*

volunteerless   eyeless   reading by the light of laser surgery

by the light cast from your eyes
Whose light whose gaze non iconic

       tender of
       call

_____
_____
_____

Phone call the 4th

            I hear anger flint   / & why not?

          I hear memory razor carver of the wrong template
template crutch   for job you've now quit

fired from   For which

I detect: Stand Up and Introduce

mothering following all eyes
dyadic dice-eyed
matia

I said guts
 rough sea

ride it out

         Forget my emmory

          address fails into this

         And who is your patron female father?

Show me the way

most probable of fat

one Ephesus tit-laden shoe fetish
                    phenomena / showing
                       Please /

warming up the wax museum

practicing the worship of egg whites   Let it burn

Our Lady of twin intention
both sides of the bread buttered

lady of the weak wrist and strong spine
Or the one who turns man to woman to fin to feather

Of the ovarian wandering suns
never to return again
every place home

                  She of the cane
               whose labors never
                    cease

abdominal one of caesarean

Of gum disease

whose tissues tear

grandmother's call, crescent arc spine, sweet ash repeat, sweet gum breeze,
seafaring ash, even ashen, Lady of lung, collapse, of august ash soap, of high
heels bending bending bending back, sailing heat's flash counter mind near
Polanski's Lady of the knife, toothless grimace, beautiful pretend invitation
publisher, she who listens sister of blood and blood blister, laughing laughing
laughing, Sweetheart

                      — honestly, I wasn't attending to you then —
sailing my own flank down to the Molos sea to fill my own lung jacket full of
June bonfire

She who had a
daughter but was
not a mother She
who could only mother

Actually we don't have to know why
Alleviated — that no
longer our job   That no
longer our oar
found far from sea

Passenger

put words on them

that's all you can do

rub them in

oddly within the found agate of

within the infinitive translation covenant that we found turning us

in one another's direction like the wrung neck of a telescope
making an about-face

so looking now from the swivel

back to embrace the many species of distance including the eradication of

measurable nameable laps between

Here there is also dispassion   .

one of the spring birds cracked into this nest

into this bursting season of brain surgery

Here at the copied key

given not fully but in intent

to the hands of the parent guarding the opening of the door

and the opening of the skull

One copy slipped through the cracks of attention's symmetry

The first the hypothesis of care while

the other awaits the new lock behind which

crucibles in the shape of books blinded in binding
stand in seeing in

surprise there is a standard to the endurable and another
that is not

within the worm cloth whose frays

come to bed

come to

If I don't know the whole story your face is the whole story

      not the guise despised or in procession

      the one I don't know handed around handed off

If I don't know the whole sight

—

—

The 8 year old's vision
Him kneeling at the foot of the bed
in the shtetl tenement
 stands in

—

If I don't know the whole year

ultra and near years introduce

When the story brokers

break

When the comments
comment upon

For you derelict satellite

wandering back through the mesh of brittle teeth

rain-stunted and kool-aid schooled in the family of

                              overbearance

        fake star in clutter sky

        up truant in spite of the orders of the pantheon

The conductor in the belfry proposes a situation

Walls of barnacle

Chairs of pearl   An underwater chamber of inner ear   We listen at the door

and so it is He   And so it is here: You children no longer childlike

You ears in need of aid
gather round and throw rice at the

and you at the sleep counter
sifting glass from sand

wipe off your faces on the holy cloth from Constantinople
on which His face once appeared

Bear witness to the presence of the features without a painter
to a letter written in his hand without hand, the cloth with which he washed
their feet, the scourge, the cane, the sponge, blood, nails, lance, robe, girdle, shoes,
sudarium of the entombment, the stone laid beneath his head . . . the robe of the
mother, the girdle, veil, shoes . . . his hand with the arm, some of his hairs . . . the
staff of Moses . . . the conductor's batons at rest forever . . . the complete head and
his chains . . . the stone on which he sat while he talked with the mob . . . emerald
gem stones like the stars that he saw in the sky . . . [There follows the account

of the blood-flecked Jew who had to free himself from suspicion of being a
murderer.]

the living dead stored their eyes here

while the blind kept in their lockdown

lent sight to the procession

songs, hymns, recipes, guttural utterings of the skin not close enough yet,
through three doors, three streets broken into more threes

days broken off from their calendars
of 3 x 4

Who could have seen the foreshadow in the wood

that brought us here

whose multiples and multiplication = each excursion into trying to
understand

icon or book icon of book
not only face but proximity

Between the tight swaddling of the infant
and the dressing of the lamb roast — between talking and taking
laying bare and generosity, between
the roiling war and the ways of our lives that were

Find me

If I escape

It is from lack of practice

       wisdomless the branch returns to
          its tree
   hold me far from habit to show

     fear's face-off with the
       nickelodeon dawn with
  the exquisite problem of repetition

Dear of the nameless

     of distraction and counter distraction

        always have been
        isn't explanation

      hereafter
       procession of ardors armor

what is abstract, the future
fleet face of the marked
only breath remains
whose hardly matters
in this we travel
laid bare

If you were not where I thought
you would be

It is because thought is too slow

Tell me everything
time-bound

Then tell me every exhale
untold

Pavilion passenger

    spacious tent

in which we turn

   so in equal and opposite nod

   car omens, fish scale skies

   offer up the sleep of birds

   while we set our clocks by the visits of bees

   you brainstem flower
   gatherer gathered

starlings show the direction of the sun

internal compass   even in dim light   across time zones
          jetlag and shift-work

we skim the shoals of hypnotoxin

Shipwreck on egg crust vomit

Even that shock serves

as passport broker

this city   as all   scene of invisible crime
and we tour the perimeter of that invisibility

Then off we go backseat sleeper

To the mobs

formations of volcanic core tower

where tour busses disgorge   at the feet

of the real eyeless stone idols

torn into Christendom

Ashamed in your gilded cameo

swollen pudgy-faced infant

Praise to your surprise

third-century-caught tribute to hunger

scanning the room in search of her

As to whisper is another

way to breathe and to not

Tutor me in impeccable run-off

You whose shoulders serve as rain

to my gutter songs, irrigation ditch movies, vacant lot taunts,
ship deck swabs

Show there is actually no sphinx other than the one

on the plinth casting complaint, no sirens but those

Breathe air-conditioned sleep terraces

Exhale the verticality of cypress

Darkness whisper light no disaster
Frailties of flesh up close now as camphor

In the morning garden a bending over
Then straddle the stonewall and collect from its neighbor

Ecstatic birds of the no-fly zone

non escort martyrs on the day cusp
blasting the inward spiral stairs
then descend through the orthodox call

You in that V that could be the sea
that could be a boat flanking swimmers of views

It is still early morning torn from drought

working off the punch card
stealing from the till

stone sleeps

not yet lit

      pent-up fire

           missing term

             rough-shod

     covenant

scarecrow mystagogy

A late sequel of frontal lobotomy

Lake of periodic temporary cessation

mouth breathing   thumb sucking   nurslings your limbs

eyewitness decadence

Coasting
as if it is news

as if continuance

whose sandman refuses flocks

nods off each time

a glass road melts

Hail tutor of night and day

cerebral cortex your absence is theirs

                           spindle

           conductive   somnolence

                        Drift

neap tide   spring tide diel diurnal

Bow

to Body Temperature   speed of response Royalty

   afternoon naps of pre-school children recall

passengers on steamer decks
   of midnight sun cruises

You were not vivid

                then

The middle voice and the
             middle distance
       hand in hand
trotting off since
       into the horizon

If his / face is the / saint it is

  also the / meeting at the cross roads

      also the unspeakable icon

        that the face can't

         show

Starling   You were wind then

                     — for S. D.

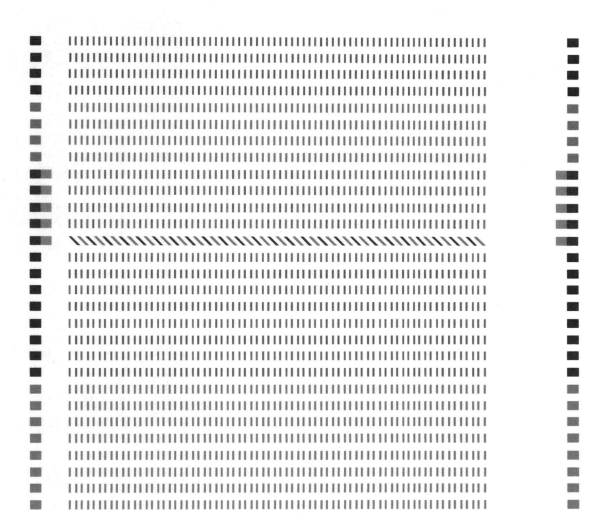

HOUSE

No, he's not inside the
house. Thunderstorm is
conjuring *tamales* in the
doorway when 13 Lord
passes and 8 more days
bring 8 calm

Popol Vuh #13, Dennis Tedlock translation

We lay on our hands
As they pass under
  we are an arbor
And their curved backs our
bread rising

while those clawed

run in and out

half blood half rain

Rest

Stocking up supplies, stories and docile be

Eat, the unconflicted   domicile

blood of the plant

midnight inventory

chameleon of forms

beckon of forms

tinker boat
toy house
box turtle sunk in the tub
pig heart in a nutshell

track and count milk lunch

Come crouch around her radiance

oranges, cunts, seaweed and
        sweet briar, cockles and a floor
      of pastry crust (sawdust)
the house made up for a ball

She wraps her lengthening vines around

A skidding augury of arms

1st 2nd 3rd degree burns
of the distant children

So fading and repeating

our motions a season
our season a resemblance to our
forbears our faces thinning leave
room for theirs

That's the house, sentimental as brick
hard as snowmelt, bright as a gas flame

Enters leaves leaves enters   breaks or putties
        the surface   Touches and names everything he
names touches, then hope itself has to reach for itself

Again, the house, so like the
seafloor
and the custody of the body
        by the body of the house

mind of rotted bone or coral or styrofoam

task on the long prairie between

holiday malady

crumb by crumb

on their behalf

What falls, flies, hastens?

swells the rib cage

of my heart

Swollen gland
skin by oil of jasmine
to cast out strep

Everything else is junk mail

Anything that thinks it escapes

lives on anti-freeze

While here through stucco

stars spill

on fever

child in flannel ferry

reaches for my hair

While their somnolent mass

drags the rafters

below sea level

Send them

to the wolverine den

gravel pit

When they come back the fanged slip
in too

road rash on the skin of the house

So delegate — eye of newt in the thermos

So awaken — dead to dream

Endure example they'll mimic

tedious appearance the shell

of the procedural versus its shattering

so nearby kept secret
uninvited inhabitants dwell in ownership

so calm
calendric passages

presto logs
      candlesticks carried from Lithuania or the lower east side

Always the cheerful pillage

sundering the rudder from its awl
telling drill mornings

outburst music
subterranean conquests

Knock in the middle of the middle of the night

pumice to bottom of bone
dead reckoning minus thinking

grey wolf rehab

Is the house a national park?

dogs guarding the borders
the boundary waters and the
boiling water guarding the borders

Shape of habitation's habit
wedding to a mind's intaglio born into indoors
What else can we want to want

Tender carnivore encounter trophy
unbridgeable embrace of both-faced
Ingest almanac kiss of days orders of use user
    grist in snapshot currency willing to consume
bodies built of weather cook in patience of
indifference

we suns extinct as the four walls we inhabit

zoo vocation   pet scrutiny   involuntary concentration

breaks the water with her dive

lost to the child
forever after equals the surface broken

Flour of fishbone
for the Mother's bones

what is commensurability

What is imaginable lodged
in the place of the child
is not mine
her face is our overlay
"this takes place in us"

If

      puberty is the first hypochondria

for girls

the house is the first illness

and fitness
full of possibility as
   punishment trophy

music box

cracked safe

re run

succumb too
at first even oven butter seems possible
fresh baked fragrant enclosure
hearth in wish honeycomb

flying seeds give air visibility

grafted to animal of plant our choice too is only air

Here under the big top where

no one looks the same for long

Of the ones eating dinner together

ages of face cleansed of face

and youth a noise of static a kind of veil

that does fall away

leaving a calla lily blaring white against

the greens of the morning garden

Therein lies the
full-bloom in the blood

inherited pre-initial events

twinned to
pogroms

so the pouring of salt on

electrocution each morning

and eventide the contours of

her life beside which may

rivers of hot ore

warm the cold blooded

who enter with the febrile

and cover us in their net

Wrap you against

Call across

the great acres

halls, rooms, stoves, locks, windows

routines made outgrown

backyard ferocity

raccoons on the sidewalk, feral cat

on the couch

permeable walls

bell weather

mixing bowl

dolmen troglodyte

What is commensurability between

dis and regulation

letter in water

who animates and reads aloud

between the minutes

Skara Brae of the stone age Orkneys as close as a sheet on skin

Perhaps he who is both faced also is *the Lord of Growing Fruit in the sky*

sip hummingbird
            inoculation
    against
Down in the locker
        do or die
sword swallowing

someone is
stowing away
    the loved one

blossoms set with fruit
rain floods and grounds the bees

You become a humble servant of the random
so illness abates you

You arrive at a dead end, you lie down
under a shower of plaster and stars

even at entry to the Undoing Days

at the bottom of the hour

where fallow talk walks the plank

happily happily truly honeyed hopefully
roulette is a shared ride
voluntarily we partake towards actions of the rose bower

endless sweetness just pours through us

And we are at its service

"birds land on my arms

a kestrel, a little falcon" white parakeets
a white cat, white stallion and later a white dog come to stay

It's true
the updraft
can
volunteer us

turn us tree upbraiding floors with our

roots

Turn us

sparrow

dust bather

nest defender

draining flowers of nectar

and I always only here lost tooth choked liver

in minutes you'll wake up

to this meal

anoint cells bones fibers

when health estranged escapes

call pull it back to brace for

handless futures

close our eyelids

ichor and starlight

sleep tandem

NOTES FROM PRE

The sea as immovable as dry land
— Ioanna Karystiani

there are wheels in her words
— William Langland

who are you
bright comet

issuing from a craven
planet

bitten off from stale bread

Set out

why

set out again
why

set out throughout
a whole life

bound to the rim
of the wheel of going

where are you who

how hail there to there

Fatata forwandred tired moon phos caught

so
accomplishes in reverse all things and at arm's length

Who are you where requirement

force of will subject to will

leave me in local relapse

there is no pure language only
        rules and their many exceptions
        on the exceptions the going

            way of why

build me a rhyme so
I can remember how   [dismember and reassemble]
we got here and climb it for
the retrace of way back   pitch it
in the cradle of traceless
origin (reverse)
in ears leavened with stand-ins

Mercy for the
troubled one and the
one in trouble
the ill one and the
one made ill by the
ill one

ure recovery from oure habits

heofonum of Pontic pioneers
trove heuones habits' trinkets

shooting star jasmine stencil
while the child wakes
bereft with desertion in her own
unknown language
misheard beforehand

Okay wandred we'll talk about it later

     Come

          now

        my tiredress

           shepherd as if jobless

So we are the enemy now   blocking their view

closed of eye   yawn ports

rife of smile // So you are the mouth of this
protectorship, where you will tell us
what sell and take us

arms from the cliff face swim the air

No nought jugglers come
joculartore with stories wringing your necks
forcing spit from wooden lips
refuse to hit or be clobbered
no choice but divulgence penance

implores from the cliff face

By the seat of grass stain or slip shod or slid ear — it doesn't matter
when you enter the water the number
of laps only breath in and extension
returning tempered in the sea forge
this evades contraction of exhaustion's nag and the
flogged animals of tether and teach

I'll remember her later

In a hollow on the
    cliff face
   way above the
drop off   lives

origin upon origin upon

                                                        pillar, pitch,

stucco, thatch

white on white moon sea

                                        duplicate place-holder agent

masses of faceless dressed up for us

curses to the standard with her correct insignias
         and spelling of armor for jousting over
         dresses fair

So we go
      Globe Stonehenge theatre ark
      enter under sun that will cross over
      thousands of heads but never strike
      the actor in the eye

Get in
      At the tower halt
      for the *Handing Over of the Password*
      from whom to whom long life sheds its
      sound of stone lions, deep moat
      shuffle warm-blooded guards

The North now
      in its luscious grace
      Heads on stakes

unwashed Elizabethans the stars of mariners   small physiques and
walled cities

           clamber close
              without way back

lunatic Baedeker

who were you bright

      scissoring hot air from air

as if climatic wish exists

and the hostelry
called and said

what more ye spinnith

to wend no nought

double negatives indwell in modern Greek and old English

juggler & joculatore respite
from the doubled deaf present

Fata

forwandred

to wend

turne No naught

at bedside

Mars and Amore

rake 1st lines

for first signs of englysh

escape wintercounts

feeding on sleep the way
tiny fish feed on a reef
On the faraway the way gamblers suckle the slot machine

Who are you where

stale and renewed return

Leave me to local relapse

a thing once seen cannot be escaped
but can be preponed

its undertow
will not abate

Amaliada of ancient olives and current quarrel
coddle what was for echo of what to do

eyes closed
on hands and knees
going forth through sewage pipes and
storm drains

A place can be
idea dreampt
don a pelt of another's life is not to befriend
maybe Antiklea and Ino showed us
how to crawl beside
how not to miss what we've misunderstood

decoy substitute trick executed against
impossibility of motion

To go back there
            will be so

one before the next

into the ice palace

riven by meltemi winds

Here to the entering

always and all the ways
            a little melting
It is time to take
on the mantle over the shoulders
it goes like the shawl of the bent
ditch diggers   feet by the fire or
cape of a nightrider
fleeing white hot
by darkness

parallel neath

She walks ahead

ambush of charred seeds

frontier Faeder fadir

hand on the knife dipped in the peanut butter
handle around future's corner
whose hand grasps the handle
was grasp always in us

accomplished   the going on the wide sea

proto   the grim of pilgrimage the age of the

search for "the companion of aftermath" — Dorn

but before beforehand

Now I've forgotten
         everything

And could go back
    like one blind
        brightly into

a former discarded life

READY

— for Sam

Nobody
knows
what
the
sleeper
knows

Magnolia hymnal

weaned of noise
lean hours
may keep you
called home

white bloom

When the trumpet of the Lord doth sound
time will be no more

Here
on the I.V.
on the
fall leaf
depart and revel
pageant
even the splendor of jello

lay back
on upholstered
air

swollen sea light
 rest
so like the other
inflated dream

You go first pilot

hand on the rip cord

    trail blazer of River Glorious

  Burn in Me Fire of

Kingdom songs

[now we are the keepers of your]

8 YEAR YAHRZEIT

little ocean rock

backyard iris burn

cloak and mettle
approach and devoid

children's height you'd never have imagined

— for my Dad

THE BIRDHANDLERS

— for Sam

Draemon

Sleep Out Loud

Not twins   Exhaustion & Sleep

Come birds — land on my arm — and
show me the rest of flight

To the birdhandlers

he left led by a dog

after years ago a walk on the beach

when he confessed to preparation

As if going hunting

he fell to the floor

Then begged to come back

to the pre-departure half shut days

Like a dog pointing

he sent the birdhandlers

to teach me how to do it

long bend of torso bandage

water the compost

till rot blooms

belief is hard to summon

in that garden

broken or jumping around like elastic on paddle ball toys

Where is captivation? — one lit-up point leading to a field of lit-up doors all
leading to magnetic flood-lit acres — Bully me again someday please

my redundant nothing   darling

Sleep now dear — the day has been long and

filled with wonder   Book of Days

no big project — just small swathes of bright

In this land they know how to take a bird
gently by the neck

a bird can land in your hair
just to wait not nest

A cutting, a slip of trunk

feed it by eyedropper

rest will increase a few minutes per day

Turn the latchkey at the back of the chest
the engine will run down

Now not alert the
spreading of fibers can begin

warm molasses milk
rove slowly
summer months cutting their teeth on wind
wander the hollows
when fall strikes a nest is ready
in the curve of the lumbar
swinging from the opposite end of
the season wheel

To track birds from the ground
You follow beneath as they shift formation You run
under leaving a footprint stencil of flight

SOME SOURCES

CODICIL

San Francisco Chronicle, Nov 23, 2001

Radio broadcast day of Rodney King verdict and LA "riots" "uprising" of April 1992

Maurice Blanchot, *The Infinite Conversation*

Disneyland Hotel paraphernalia

My Father's will

— Written between April 22, 2001 and December 2002
   (U.S. announces plan to invade Iraq)

CIRCADIA

Loring Danforth, *Firewalking and Religious Healing: The Anastenaria of Greece and the American Firewalking Movement*

Hans Belting, *Likeness and Presence: A History of the Image before Art*

HOUSE

"Let us seek instead an anti-writing against the seductive illusions of the 'beauty' of nature."
— Paul Shepard, *Others: How Animals Make Us Human*

The hymns chanted in the Greek church are called "oikoi," houses, that are made of sound and movement, meditation and praise

NOTES FROM PRE

Ioanna Karystiani, *The Jasmine Isle*

William Langland, *Piers Plowman*

"Of course there is actually no such thing as travel. So they say. There is nothing but a *Voyage autour de ma Chambre*, meaning *de tout ce que je suis*, even in a *tour du monde*."
— Dorothy Richardson, *Dawn's Left Hand*, from *Pilgrimage* IV

Chaucer, *The Parliament of the Fowls*

Fata short for Fatata woman of supernatural powers

"…an idea is a thing seen…"
— Robert Duncan, *The Sweetness and Greatness of Dante's Divine Comedy*

READY

July 25th morning: "This is a poem I made up — It's not amen yet."
— Sam Hurst

THE BIRDHANDLERS

Draemon = Old English — to dream and make music